# Power to the People

# *Our* Government and Citizenship

SPIRIT
of America®

# Power to the People

## HOW WE ELECT THE PRESIDENT AND OTHER OFFICIALS

*By Kevin Cunningham*

*Content Adviser: David R. Smith, PhD, Academic Advisor and Adjunct*
*Assistant Professor of History, The University of Michigan, Ann Arbor, Michigan*

*The Child's World*
*Chanhassen, Minnesota*

10

# Power to the People

*Published in the United States of America by The Child's World®*
PO Box 326 • Chanhassen, MN 55317-0326 • 800-599-READ • www.childsworld.com

*Acknowledgments*
The Child's World®: Mary Berendes, Publishing Director

Editorial Directions, Inc.:E. Russell Primm, Editorial Director; Pam Rosenberg, Line Editor; Katie Marsico, Associate Editor; Judi Shiffer, Associate Editor and Library Media Specialist; Matthew Messbarger, Editorial Assistant; Susan Hindman, Copy Editor; Lucia Raatma, Proofreader; Judith Frisbee, Peter Garnham, and Olivia Nellums, Fact Checkers; Tim Griffin/IndexServ, Indexer; Cian Loughlin O'Day, Photo Researcher; Linda S. Koutris, Photo Selector

*Photo*
Cover: Cover/frontispiece: Erik Freeland/Corbis Saba.
Interior: AP/Wide World: 15 (Darryl Webb), 16 (Sandy Macys), 22 (Spencer Tirey), 23 (Victoria Arocho), 26 (Greg Wahl-Stevens); Bettmann/Corbis: 6, 8, 17, 20; Corbis: 11 (Flip Schulke), 13 (Brooks Kraft), 19 (Ralph-Finn Hestoft), 28 (Alan Schein Photography); Getty Images/Hulton|Archive: 7, 10; Getty Images/Stone/Andy Sacks: 24.

*Library of Congress Cataloging-in-Publication Data*
Cunningham, Kevin, 1966–
    Power to the people : how we elect the president and other officials / by Kevin Cunningham.
        p. cm. — (Our government and citizenship)
    Includes index.
    ISBN 1-59296-322-6 (library bound : alk. paper) 1. Elections—United States—Juvenile literature. I. Title. II. Series.
    JK1978.C86 2005
    324.6'0973—dc22                                    2004007202

# *Contents*

## Chapter ONE

# The Idea of Democracy

MORE THAN 2,000 YEARS AGO, THE ANCIENT GREEKS practiced a form of democracy. So did the ancient Romans. A thousand years ago, people in Iceland started a **democracy.** The idea of democracy goes back a long time.

*The ancient Greeks practiced a form of democracy thousands of years ago.*

Voting is a democracy's most basic right. It allows citizens to choose their own representatives for all kinds of government positions—from local school board members to the president of the United States. Democracy is a tremendously powerful idea. In 1776, the hope for democracy drove American colonists to fight the British, who had the most powerful military in the world. Even today, people around the world still risk their lives for the right to vote.

"For our government is not copied from those of our neighbors: we are an example to them rather than they to us. Our constitution is named a democracy, because it is in the hands not of the few but of the many."

It's easy to imagine Thomas Jefferson saying these proud words. Or Abraham Lincoln. Or modern politicians trying to sound like Jefferson or Lincoln. But these words weren't spoken by an American. Nor were they talking about the United States. These words were spoken by Pericles, an ancient Greek government leader. He said them in a speech more than 2,000 years before the American Revolution (1775–1783). When Pericles gave this speech in 431 B.C., his city, Athens, was home to the world's first democracy.

*Pericles was born in about 495 B.C. in the city of Athens, Greece.*

Democracy in Athens was very different than democracy in the United States today. For one thing, only about 16 percent of the citizens of Athens could vote. People who were not allowed to vote included women, slaves, non-Athenians, and anyone with a non-Athenian parent.

Athenian democracy was different in other ways as well. Voters in Athens did not elect others to repre-sent them. Instead, they took part directly in the democracy. They did this by meeting in assemblies. In the assemblies, the citizens of Athens would propose **legislation** and vote on it. If the voters in the assemblies approved the legislation, then it was sent to the Council of Five Hundred. This was a group made up of 500 voters chosen completely at random. Any voter might be on the Council of Five Hundred. If the Council of Five Hundred approved the legislation, it went to a panel of 10 generals. Once the generals approved it, the legislation became law.

In time, Athens collapsed, but its democratic ideas proved powerful enough to echo for centuries. The desire for democracy returned during the Age of Enlightenment in the late 1600s and 1700s. In the Enlightenment, people began thinking about the world in a new way. Scientists had started to discover the rules that governed nature. Enlightenment thinkers had a great respect for human beings and their ability to think logically. Because of this, they believed that people should have a say in their government.

In the 1700s, that was an unusual idea. For centuries, people had believed that God gave kings the right to govern. If God wanted King George in charge of the American colonies, what did it matter what the colonists thought? Some people feared that if regular people were allowed a strong say in their govern-

*John Locke was an English philosopher whose ideas influenced the authors of the U.S. Constitution.*

ment, society would fall apart. They claimed that average people lacked the wisdom and common sense to lead a nation.

But the people living in the British colonies in North America had some say in their government from very early on. A **legislature** was created in 1619 in the Jamestown Colony in Virginia. This legislature was an annual meeting of representatives called burgesses. This House of Burgesses survived until 1776, when it became the House of Delegates. It still exists today.

The colonists fought for their independence from Great Britain in part because they wanted more say in their government. They fought for the idea of democracy. Once they had won the revolution, they had to decide what form that democracy would take. They needed a **constitution.**

Leaders of the former colonies met in the summer of 1787 in Philadelphia, Pennsylvania, to work out a constitution. Some of the people who met in Philadelphia were inspired by the example of ancient Greece. But they knew that Athenian-style democracy would not work in the United States. The country was simply too big to have every voter proposing and voting on new laws. Instead, they decided that the country should be a **republic.**

When the Constitution was written, "voters" did not include all Americans. Only white males who owned land got the right to vote. This was

▶ Colonial leaders called the Constitutional Convention of 1787 to revise the Articles of Confederation. This was the first document that outlined the government of the United States during the time of the Revolutionary War. It soon became clear that instead of revising the Articles of Confederation, the new country needed a new form of government and the U.S. Constitution was written.

▶ In 1920, the Nine-
teenth Amendment
gave women the right
to vote, but only
about 49 percent of
women used the right
in the 1920 presiden-
tial election.

oddly similar to the system in Athens 2,000 years earlier.

The men involved in shaping the Constitution believed it took intelligence, education, and common sense to take part in a democracy. They believed that women, African-Americans, and Native Americans lacked those things. Strong prejudices guided these early leaders.

As for the rule about owning land, taking part in a democracy required time and energy to learn about issues. In the America of 1787, only property owners—who had others working for them—had that kind of time. American leaders also thought the property rule was a good way to keep regular people—who were considered by leaders to be untrustworthy—from voting in bad leaders. Many soldiers who had fought in the American Revolution lacked property. This rule left them wondering what they had fought for.

The rule remained in place for decades. And

*In the 1700s, many American leaders thought only men who owned property and could afford to have others working for them had time to participate in government matters.*

for many long years, women, African-Americans, and others endured threats and violence as they tried to get the right to vote. It was not until the second half of the 20th century that all adult citizens had the right to vote. Finally, American democracy was for all the people.

IT TOOK TIME, AND CHANGES TO THE CONSTITUTION, BEFORE ALL AMERICANS had the right to vote. The rule about having to own property more or less went out by the 1840s.

After the Civil War freed enslaved African-Americans, the Constitution was changed. The Fifteenth Amendment, which went into effect in 1870, granted African-Americans the right to vote.

A few states gave women the right to vote in the late 19th century. But in most places, women trying to get the vote suffered insults and threats. It was not until 1920 that the Nineteenth Amendment gave all women the right to vote.

Despite the Fifteenth Amendment, many African-Americans, especially in the South, were kept from voting well into the 20th century. A pattern of threats, tests, and taxes bullied blacks and poor whites into staying away from the ballot box. The Civil Rights Act of 1964 finally put an end to that.

# Who Is Elected?

▶ Jesse Ventura was born in Minneapolis, Minnesota, on July 15, 1951. He served in the Navy during the Vietnam War and had a successful career as a professional wrestler. When he retired from wrestling in 1984, he began a career as an actor. Ventura also worked as a radio talk show host. He was elected mayor of Brooklyn Park, Minnesota, in 1990, and served as mayor of that city until 1995.

THE UNITED STATES OPERATES UNDER A TWO-PARTY system. Today, those two parties are the Democrats and the Republicans. That's the way it's been since the late 1850s, when the Republican Party rose out of the ruins of the old Whig Party.

**Candidates** from the two parties compete on Election Day. Occasionally, a third-party candidate or an independent without an official party makes the ballot. These candidates lack the money and organizational power and structure of the Democrats and Republicans. Because of that, they usually don't get many votes. But once in a while they do. Ross Perot ran for president as an independent in 1992. He won almost 20 million votes. In 1998, Jesse Ventura of the Reform Party became governor of Minnesota. Members of the Green Party have recently won local elections in many states.

Voters elect candidates to a wide variety of national, state, and local offices. Presidential elections have the biggest **turnout.** Elections with only local races usually draw the fewest voters.

⁓

In national elections, voters decide who will represent them in Washington, D.C. They vote for the president and for members of Congress.

Without a doubt, the **campaign** for president is the loudest, most expensive contest in the land. For months and sometimes even longer, the candidates travel around the country making speeches. They appear on magazine covers and the Internet, in TV ads and newspaper articles. Everyone who can vote can cast a ballot for president.

*George W. Bush (center) faces a cheering crowd with his wife Laura at his side as he accepts the Republican nomination for president in 2000.*

The Senate has 100 members, two from each state. Voters in each state elect their senators to six-year terms. It was not always this way. In the original Constitution, state legislatures chose the senators. This is because the people who wrote the Constitution felt uneasy about too much democracy. They thought the Senate should be filled with wise legislators who looked at problems logically. The House of Representatives would be filled with those who more closely represented the people. In 1913, the Constitution was finally changed so that voters elected senators.

There are 435 members of the House of Representatives. They represent districts in their states that have been determined by population. Each district includes about 600,000 people. A state such as Wyoming that has a small population sends only one representative to Congress. California, on the other hand, has 53 representatives.

Over time, population across the country shifts. Some states gain a lot of people, while others might lose people. So every 10 years, the seats in the House are divided up again to reflect these changes. If a lot of people moved to a state, it may gain one, two, or even more representatives.

To the people who wrote the Constitution, the House was the real example of democracy in the national government. House members are closest to the people they represent. They fight for the interests of the people in their district. They work hard to get money for projects that benefit people in their home district. Representatives serve two-year terms.

The race for governor is usually the most visible state race. A governor acts as "president" of that state. She or he suggests what the state budget should be and sometimes proposes new laws. The governor also has the power to reject legislation passed by the state legislature. Different states have different rules on how long a governor serves. Usually it's four years, but in Vermont and New Hampshire, the governor has a two-year term. Every registered voter who lives in the state can vote for governor.

State legislatures serve as the Congress of a state. Like the U.S. Congress, most state legislatures have a senate and a house of representatives. Each voter lives in a district that has one state senator and one representative. Only Nebraska gets by with a legislature having just one chamber. State senators and state representatives serve two- to four-year terms, depending on the state.

Voters have a say in who runs your city or town. In many places, they choose a mayor, who is like a

*Members of the Arizona state legislature at work.*

"president" of the city. In some places, voters also elect some kind of town council. The town council is the legislature of the city. The size of the council can vary. In a small town, it might be 5 people, while in Chicago, Illinois, it's 50 people. Sometimes only the council is elected. Then the council either runs the town as a group or hires a manager to act as a sort of mayor. The length of terms for mayors and city council members varies. In most cities, voters also choose members of the library board, the zoning board, and other offices.

Forty-eight of the 50 U.S. states are divided into counties. Voters in a county are asked to choose countywide officials. These officials can include everything from school board members to the dogcatcher to the sheriff.

*Citizens at a town meeting in Vermont listen to a member of the town council.*

16

THROUGHOUT AMERICAN HISTORY, THERE HAVE BEEN TWO MAJOR political parties. But from time to time, a third party crops up. Third parties often focus on a small number of issues they feel are being ignored.

In the mid-1850s, the American Party—nicknamed the Know-Nothings—worked to keep immigrants from coming to the United States. They got their nickname because when they were asked about what they did, they were secretive and said they "knew nothing." Former Republican president Theodore Roosevelt (below) ran as the Bull Moose (or Progressive) candidate in the 1912 presidential election. The party got its name when Roosevelt, asked about his chances, said he felt "as strong as a bull moose." The 1948 presidential election saw the States' Rights candidate Strom Thurmond get more than 1 million votes campaigning against civil rights.

Most third parties have a hard time surviving. Unlike the Republicans and Democrats, third parties lack the huge organizations needed to find volunteers, run campaigns, and raise funds.

But they keep trying. After all, the Republican Party is an example of a successful third party. Since replacing the Whigs in the 1850s, the Republicans have been half of the country's two-party system.

## Chapter THREE

# The Presidential Election

RUDE. NOISY. THRILLING. NASTY. EMPOWERING. Exhausting. A presidential election is all that and more. Since George Washington retired in 1797, the race has attracted politicians, generals, businessmen, and more than one fool. The winner makes a lot of enemies and ages before our eyes. But the prize is irresistible: the most powerful political office in the country and a chance to make history.

To choose their presidential candidate, the Democrats and Republicans hold statewide elections called primaries. The primaries begin in January of an election year and run through early summer. A primary is a voter's first chance to declare a choice for a party's presidential candidate.

Often there are several candidates to choose from. These candidates organize staffs, try to raise money, and hit the campaign trail. They speak to groups, give interviews, make promises, and kiss a lot of babies. Their goal is to win votes.

Whoever wins the most votes wins the most delegates. Delegates are people who go to the party convention, or political meeting, later in the year and vote for the candidate. Each state gets a certain number of delegates based on its population. After the primary election, the state's delegates are divided up according to the percentage of the vote each candidate won. For example, if a candidate wins 25 percent of her party's vote in a state primary, then she will win 25 percent of that state's delegates.

If a president is running for reelection, his party primary often means little. Nowadays, it is unusual for someone to run against an **incumbent.** It was different in the past. As recently as 1980, Senator Edward Kennedy challenged President Jimmy Carter in the Democratic primary. More and more, though, the parties try to get their supporters behind an

*Delegates at the 1992 Democratic National Convention show their support for candidate Bill Clinton.*

incumbent as soon as possible. That way, all their energy can be focused on defeating the other party.

~~~

Today, delegates, party leaders, and everyone else arrive at the convention knowing who the candidate will be. However, up until the 1960s, conventions could be dramatic. Back then, delegates could vote for whomever they wanted. Sometimes two candidates each had a lot of support. They would have to give speeches, makes promises, and work out behind-the-scenes deals to try to convince delegates to support them. At the 1924 Democratic convention, delegates voted 103 times before deciding on John W. Davis.

*John W. Davis was born in Clarksburg, West Virginia, in 1873. Republican Calvin Coolidge soundly defeated him in the 1924 presidential election.*

Such a battle would never happen now. These days, delegates are tied to a certain candidate. Everyone knows who has the most delegates before the convention begins. Sometimes choosing a vice presidential candidate provides drama. But mostly, the conventions are just big shows meant to inspire party members and give the candidates a chance to introduce themselves and their ideas to the country. Above all, the party wants to put on its best face. Party leaders control everything from the chants and colorful signs to the speeches. Their main goal is for the voters to come away thinking that their candidate should lead the country.

＊＊＊

Now comes the real drama. Two candidates, each backed by thousands of supporters and millions of dollars, face off for the presidency.

The campaign traditionally gets rolling after Labor Day. This is when the candidates go into overdrive appearing across the country and when voters begin to pay close attention. The candidates face the kind of attention usually reserved for celebrities. Voters, journalists, and experts go over every word they say. They ask questions about a candidate's ideas and look at a candidate's past. Often the media picks apart every little gesture the candidate makes. Sometimes they even comment on hairstyles and clothes, just as with celebrities.

For voters, making an informed decision means listening, reading, thinking, and even arguing. Newspapers, magazines, TV, and the Internet make a huge amount of information available. Is Candidate Smith smart enough for the job? Honest enough? Will his policies take the country in a good direction? How will he protect the environment? What does he think of school prayer? Women's rights?

The advisers running campaigns are experts in using colorful phrases and clever TV ads to connect

## Interesting Fact

▶ Candidates John F. Kennedy and Richard M. Nixon made history during the 1960 presidential election campaign. They appeared in a series of four televised debates—the first debates between presidential candidates ever broadcast live on national TV.

with voters and to make the other candidate look bad. Informed voters have to see through these tactics. They have to figure out what's real and what really matters.

The candidates spend endless hours in front of the cameras. Meanwhile, behind the scenes, their supporters raise money, pass out fliers, and post comments on the Internet. Signs go up in yards all across the country. People wear pins to show support for their candidate.

As Election Day approaches, a blizzard of ads fills TV and radio. **Polls** are released showing which candidate is favored. If the election is close, as it was in 2000, everything becomes more intense. There are more speeches, more news, more ads.

Then, finally, it's Election Day. The candidates and journalists and consultants are done. Now it is up to the voters. Who will be president?

*Former president Clinton during an interview in 1992. Candidates spend a lot of time in front of the camera during a presidential campaign.*

22

WHO CHOOSES THE PRESIDENT? VOTERS DO—SORT OF. THE PRESIDENT IS officially chosen by the Electoral College. The Electoral College is not a school; it's a collection of delegates.

Under the Electoral College system set up in the U.S. Constitution, each state gets a certain number of "electors," or people chosen to cast a state's vote for president (such as the Rhode Island electors being sworn in by the governor, below). That number equals a state's House members plus its Senate members. A candidate needs more than half the electoral votes to win. If no one candidate gets more than half the electoral votes, then the House of Representatives decides who will be president.

On Election Day, the candidate who wins the most votes in any given state wins *all* of that state's electoral votes. In 2000, the official count in Florida showed George W. Bush winning 537 more votes than Al Gore. That meant that Bush got all 25 of Florida's electoral votes—and the presidency. Yet nation-wide, Gore received 500,000 more votes than Bush. It didn't matter. Bush had more electoral votes, so Bush won.

Many people call that unfair. Why, they ask, do we keep a system designed centuries ago that doesn't respect the citizen's votes?

Those in favor of the Electoral College say it keeps our system stable. Those opposed call it undemocratic. Because it would take a change in the Constitution to get rid of the Electoral College, chances are it's here to stay.

## Chapter FOUR

# Doing Your Part

THE HEALTH OF A DEMOCRACY DEPENDS ON PEOPLE taking part in it. People elected to office have a great deal of influence over laws and society. People involved in the political system influence those who are elected to office. Cast a vote for (or against) a candidate, and both candidates listen. Don't vote, and neither the candidates nor the parties will care what you think. It's that simple. Both the Democrats and Republicans are in the business of winning elections. To win, they need votes. They alter their policies to please voters. Non-voters mean nothing to them.

Politics affect everyone, including people who hate politics. Even if you're too young to vote, politicians make decisions

*Voters sign in and vote on election day.*

about your life. They decide how much money to spend on school lunches, where you can skateboard, what time you have to be inside at night. If you care about any law or government policy, you care enough to take part. There are many ways to do this.

Voting is basic. For just a few minutes almost every year, voters get a say in how society works. Each vote can influence what happens in your town and in your country. If Candidate Brown for mayor favors a new mall and Candidate Black is against it, voters will help decide whether that mall gets built.

Each state makes it own voting laws. In general, the following rules apply across the country:

- Voters must be U.S. citizens.
- Voters must be at least 18 years old.
- Voters must have lived in the state where they are registered to vote for a certain amount of time (often 30 days).
- Voters cannot be in prison.
- Voters cannot be mentally ill (as determined by a judge).
- Voters cannot claim the right to vote in another state.

Voter registration laws vary. In most states, people must register before Election Day. During an election year, voters can sometimes register at tables that are set up at schools and in stores. In some states, voters can register when they get their driver's licenses.

▸ If no presidential candidate wins more than half the electoral votes, the House of Representatives decides the election. This has happened three times. In 1800, the House chose Thomas Jefferson over Aaron Burr. In 1824, Andrew Jackson lost to John Quincy Adams despite having more votes. And in 1877, a special commission created by Congress gave the presidency to Rutherford B. Hayes over Samuel Tilden after a disputed vote count.

25

*You don't have to be 18 years old to ring doorbells and let people know why you think they should vote for your favorite candidate.*

All they have to do is fill out a short form. A few weeks later, voters will receive registration cards in the mail.

In Idaho, Maine, Minnesota, New Hampshire, Wisconsin, and Wyoming, voters can register on Election Day. In North Dakota, people don't even need to register. They just show up on election day and vote.

Voting is easy. Voting places open early in the morning and stay open into the evening. All employers must allow their employees time to vote. It's the law. Usually, even when there's a line, it doesn't take more than 20 minutes to vote.

Political campaigns need helping hands. Volunteers can participate a little: They can put a sign in a window or organize a get-together at a coffeehouse where people can discuss a candidate. Volunteers can also participate a lot: They can raise money or work on a candidate's speeches.

The best thing about volunteering is you don't have to be 18 years old to do it. Even if you're not up to writing speeches (yet), campaigns always need help stuffing envelopes or handing out fliers. It's great experience for those interested in politics as a career.

And here's a tip: small races and new candidates need the most help. Be reliable and upbeat, and you can make a real impact.

Unless you get a very big allowance, donating money may be tough for you. But the truth is that money plays a huge role in U.S. elections. A person can contribute money to candidates for any office, although there are rules about how much. Candidates for president can raise millions of dollars in a single night. But in a local race, even $25 can go a long way.

A single voter has a little power, but a group of voters acting together can sometimes really get a politician's attention. Thousands of groups are organized around one issue or a set of issues. These are called special interest groups. Some groups focus on lowering taxes, while others work to protect the environment or freedom of speech. These groups pressure politicians to pass laws supporting their views. They donate money to candidates who believe what they believe. Big groups such as the National Rifle Association and the Sierra Club can consistently get results.

Newspapers, magazines, cable TV, radio, the Internet—never before have voters had access to so much information. Use them all when forming an opinion on an issue. Dig up facts. Find out what experts say. Don't be afraid to think for yourself.

## Interesting Fact

▸ There are limits on how much an individual person or company can contribute to an election campaign. To get around these limits, people organize political action committees, or PACs. These groups can be formed by corporations, labor unions, or any other special interest group. By soliciting contributions from many individuals, PACs can raise large amounts of money for their favorite candidates.

Only 27 percent of Americans eligible to vote elected George W. Bush to be president in 2000. Almost half of the people who could have voted didn't vote at all. In fact, more than 50 million of them never even registered. And the presidential election is the election people care about most!

Be a part of the half that votes. Wars were fought for democracy. Even today, people around the world are risking their lives for it. Make your voice heard. And—when you are old enough—vote.

## Why People Don't Vote

VOTER TURNOUT IN THE UNITED STATES IS AMONG THE LOWEST IN THE WORLD. Voting has been declining since about 1960, but voter turnout has really gone downhill since the late 1980s.

Americans offer a lot of reasons for not voting:

- The presidential campaign is long and boring.
- They're disgusted with the money and shallowness in politics.
- They don't identify with one party or the other.
- They believe parties respond only to "special interests" instead of regular people.
- They're just not interested.
- Busy lives and careers don't allow them time to get involved.

*431 B.C.*　Pericles gives a speech explaining why Athens's democratic system is better than other political systems.

*1619*　The House of Burgesses, the first legislature in the American colonies, is founded in the Jamestown Colony.

*1787*　American leaders meet in Philadelphia, Pennsylvania, to work out the U.S. Constitution.

*1788*　New Hampshire becomes the ninth state to approve the U.S. Constitution, making it law.

*1789*　The Electoral College elects George Washington the first U.S. president on February 2; the Constitution takes effect on March 3.

*1848*　The first Women's Rights Convention is held in Seneca Falls, New York; the movement to allow women to vote grows out of the meeting.

*1870*　Congress passes the Fifteenth Amendment, guaranteeing the right to vote to all U.S. citizens regardless of "race, color, or previous condition of servitude."

*1877*　The House of Representatives selects Rutherford B. Hayes as president over Samuel Tilden, the winner of the popular vote.

*1913*　Congress passes the Seventeenth Amendment, which gives voters the power to directly elect their senators.

*1920*　Congress passes the Nineteenth Amendment, guaranteeing women the right to vote.

*1965*　The Civil Rights Act, along with the Twenty-Fourth Amendment, tears down laws barring African-Americans from voting.

*1971*　Congress passes the Twenty-Sixth Amendment, lowering the voting age from 21 to 18.

*1992*　Independent candidate Ross Perot gets almost 20 million votes in the presidential election.

*1998*　Third-party candidate Jesse Ventura becomes governor of Minnesota.

*2000*　The Supreme Court awards Florida's Electoral College delegates to George W. Bush, giving him the presidency over Al Gore, the winner of the popular vote.

**campaign (kam-PANE)**

A campaign is an organized effort to win an election. The presidential campaign is the most expensive campaign in the United States.

**candidates (KAN-duh-dates)**

Candidates are people running for office in an election. In 2000, George W. Bush was the Republican candidate for president.

**constitution (kon-stuh-TOO-shun)**

A constitution is a document outlining the structure and basic laws of a government. The U.S. Constitution was written in 1787.

**democracy (di-MAH-kruh-see)**

In a democracy, the citizens elect the members of a government. The United States is a democracy.

**incumbent (in-KUM-bunt)**

An incumbent is someone who currently holds office. Often, no one runs against the incumbent during the presidential primary.

**legislation (le-juh-SLAY-shun)**

Legislation is a rule or law that is put up for a vote by a government. Congress writes and passes new legislation.

**legislature (LEH-juh-slay-chur)**

A legislature is a group that makes laws. Congress is the legislature of the U.S. government.

**polls (POLZ)**

Polls ask voters which candidate they plan to vote for in an upcoming election. News organizations often take polls to try to determine what voters are thinking.

**republic (re-PUH-blik)**

A republic is a type of government where voters elect representatives who are supposed to stand up for their interests and needs. The United States is a republic.

**turnout (TURN-out)**

The turnout is the number of people who take part in an election. Voter turnout in the United States has declined since the late 1980s.

### Books

Donovan, Sandra. *Running for Office: A Look at Political Campaigns.* Minneapolis: Lerner Publications, 2004.

Gutman, Dan. *Landslide: A Kid's Guide to U.S. Elections.* New York: Aladdin Paperbacks, 2000.

St. George, Judith, and David Small (illustrator). *So You Want to Be President?* New York: Philomel Books, 2000.

Sanders, Mark C. *Your Right to Vote.* Austin, Tex.: Steadwell Books, 2000.

### Web sites

Visit our home page for lots of links about elections:
**http://www.childsworld.com/links.html**

*Note to Parents, Teachers, and Librarians:*
We routinely verify our Web links to make sure they're safe, active sites—so encourage your readers to check them out!

### Places to Visit or Contact
**Democratic National Committee**
*To write for information about the Democratic Party and what it stands for*
430 South Capitol Street SE
Washington, DC 20003
212/863-2000

**Republican National Committee**
*To write for information about the Republican Party and what it stands for*
310 First Street SE
Washington, DC 20003
212/863-8500

# Index

## About the Author

KEVIN CUNNINGHAM IS AN AUTHOR AND TRAVEL WRITER. HE STUDIED journalism and history at the University of Illinois at Urbana. His other books include *Condoleezza Rice: Educator and Presidential Adviser, The Declaration of Independence,* and *The U.S. Congress: Who Represents You.* He lives in Chicago.